B & B EDUCATIONAL ADVANCEMENT & PUBLICATIONS INC.
1407 FORD STREET, GOLDEN, CO 80401
TELEPHONE: 866-930-5140
WEBSITE: WWW.BBEAPUBLICATIONS.COM
ISBN: 978-1-937065-00-3

CRACKING THE SYSTEM

STUDY GUIDE FOR TEENS

This book is a "must-have" study guide for teens who want to get organized, stay organized and succeed in school. Written by a teacher and parent of teens, Cracking the System gives you the inside information you are looking for!

By Luann Swim

2012

Cracking the System: Study Skills for Teens
By Luann Swim

ABOUT THE AUTHOR: *Luann Swim has taught students from preschool to college age, in classrooms, one-on-one, and in after-school programs, using concepts learned in graduate work at the University of Colorado at Denver. But with a B.S. in Horticulture from the University of Wisconsin, Madison she also has years of work experience, from production to sales. She is perhaps proudest to be in her final years of the "Graduate University of Learning to Parent (GULP☐)", with children in both college and high school. All this experience working with both adults and kids has given her a unique perspective regarding what it takes to be successful in both school and the workplace*

Cracking the System: Study Skills for Teens
By Luann Swim

TABLE OF CONTENTS

Study Guide for Teens: How to Get Organized & Succeed
By Luann Swim

ABOUT THE AUTHOR	1
TABLE OF CONTENTS:	2
INTRODUCTION	4
IT'S ALL ON YOU	5
Own It	6
Go for It	6
Track It	9
Celebrate Your Success	13
ORGANIZATION	15
Be prepared	15
Using a planner	16
Tools of the trade	20

Cracking the System: Study Skills for Teens
By Luann Swim

Transport & storage:backpacks/ lockers	24
Developing a system	26
CLASSROOM STRATEGIES	**27**
Be prepared	27
Active listening	30
Note-taking strategies	31
Using a planner	36
HOMEWORK HELPS	**37**
Be prepared and use your planner	37
Time and place	40
CSIQ	42
Help! I don't get it!	43
Turning it in	45
TESTS	**48**
Be prepared	48
Using a planner	48
Study tips	49
Memory tips	50
CONCLUSION	**55**

Cracking the System: Study Skills for Teens
By Luann Swim

INTRODUCTION

Do you sometimes feel like you're missing something when it comes to succeeding at school? Part of a successful school experience is understanding and negotiating the ins and outs of the school/educational system. This book, written for teens from middle to high school, will help you navigate through getting organized, taking notes, completing homework, and taking tests.

YOU, however, are the single biggest factor in your future success in school. Yes, your school, its curriculum, and teachers are important but you are the determining factor. Learning is an active process with you as the director; you have control over the funnel!

Cracking the System: Study Skills for Teens
By Luann Swim

Young children need to learn everything. (After all, we start out pretty helpless in life and wouldn't make it too far on our own if we stayed that way!) But by your teens, you start to feel pretty smart and question the usefulness of things you must learn in school. This questioning is a sign of maturity but you still have a long way to go. School needs to be your full-time job and you have incredible influence on what and how much you learn. So it shouldn't be too surprising that the first section of this book is all about motivation and attitude. Once we've vaulted that hurdle its time to talk strategy: how do you come up with a plan to succeed that works for you? That's where we will look at ways to "Crack the System," getting it to work in your favor, instead of against you.

IT'S ALL ON YOU

OWN IT!

Do you think you just don't have what it takes to be a "good" student? Are your teachers not fair or

Cracking the System: Study Skills for Teens
By Luann Swim

don't like you? Do your parents forget to remind you to do your homework? Do your classmates talk to you so much that you can't concentrate in class? Did your dog eat your homework?

I'm sure that you can think of a million more excuses that you or your friends use for not succeeding in school. Or perhaps you have some more serious challenges: parents who work all the time, only one or no parents, lack of money, an unsafe neighborhood, or friends that pressure you to do things you know aren't right. You can search the web to find scores of famous people who overcame their learning disabilities or life challenges and succeeded in their chosen fields. But these success stories have one thing in common: hard work. Novelist John Irving, who didn't realize he had a learning disability, knew it would take him twice as long to finish his assignments as it did others. Even Michael Jordan was cut from his high school basketball team. During his career he lost plenty of games and missed thousands of shots. But he said,

Cracking the System: Study Skills for Teens
By Luann Swim

"I have failed over and over and over again in my life. And that is why I succeed... Obstacles don't have to stop you. If you run into a wall, don't turn around and give up. Figure out how to climb it, go through it, or work around it." Educational researchers have even found that reinforcing and providing recognition for effort (hard work) can lead to a 29% increase in achievement scores. So, I guess the next thing you need to ask yourself is am I willing to put forth the effort? If not, this book can't help you. If so, then read on.

    It is time to accept responsibility for your own success or failure. As long as you keep blaming someone or something else, you will never achieve your true potential. At this stage in your life, you probably wish for more independence and more choices. This is a great place to start! Independence usually needs to be earned and taking charge of your own education shows everyone, teachers, parents, and future employers, that you can accept responsibility and act on it.

Cracking the System: Study Skills for Teens
By Luann Swim

So how does this apply to school and study skills? First, you need to set some goals for yourself. Then, you need to monitor your own progress. And finally, you need to reward yourself for actually meeting (or exceeding) your set goals.

Read on if you are ready to get started...

GO FOR IT

Hey, great! You've decided that you are responsible for your own success (or failure)! Now what? It's time to set some reasonable goals. What makes a goal reasonable? It should be something that you can realistically expect to accomplish in the time allowed. If you are failing 3 of your classes now, is it reasonable to expect that you will be on the honor roll at the end of the semester? No. But, it is reasonable that within the next week you will meet with at least one teacher and develop a plan to improve your grade in that class.

Each situation is different and you will need to set a goal or goals that work for you. Even if you are

Cracking the System: Study Skills for Teens
By Luann Swim

accepting responsibility for your own learning, it's OK to ask for help. In fact, if you want to improve, it would probably be a good idea to get someone else's opinion: parents, teachers, or your counselor. Here are just a few suggestions to get you thinking:

- Complete, and turn in, all my homework next week
- Bring up my history grade from a C to a B in the next month
- Pay attention and take notes in Science for the next 2 weeks

Now, think of your own goal or goals and write them down here. State your goal specifically and then identify the time needed or date to complete it.

GOAL	DATE/TIME NEEDED

Cracking the System: Study Skills for Teens
By Luann Swim

Some of your goals may need to be broken down into manageable tasks. For example, if you want to raise your history grade in a month, you will need to break this goal into specific tasks, most likely with your teacher's help. There might be homework to be completed, reading to be done, and studying for a quiz or test. Most teachers can help you anticipate your work load so you can fit it in with all the other things you want to do. Schedule time for each one in your planner and then check it off when complete. (More about getting organized, using class time wisely, homework, and testing tips in the rest of the book!)

Now that you have identified a goal or goals, let's talk about how you will check up on yourself or monitor your progress.

TRACK IT

Since **you** are responsible for your achieving your goals, you will need to check on your progress. Many schools have an online program that allows you to check your grades, attendance, etc. This is

Cracking the System: Study Skills for Teens
By Luann Swim

your first stop! Get in the habit of checking this program several times a week.

If the online grade book shows a missing assignment that you think you turned in, first look for it in your desk, binders, folders, backpack, and locker. (Most kids who insist they've turned in assignments find them somewhere else!) Once you've looked everywhere, and then looked again, either turn it in, even if late, or talk to your teacher ASAP. It is possible that your assignment was misfiled. If it cannot be found, do the assignment again! Even if you cannot get credit for it, this will show your teacher that you are acknowledging that accidents happen and you are willing to go the extra mile. (If this happens more than once, spend some extra time reading the chapters on Organization and Homework Helps. You probably need some help getting organized.)

Are you unhappy about a grade you received on an important assignment or project? First, go back to the directions or rubric and try to figure out why the grade was given and what you could have done to make it better. Then, if you are willing to put in some more effort, make an appointment with your teacher to discuss your work. Explain to your teacher what you have discovered about your work, ask for confirmation or suggestions, and then ask if you can make these changes to improve your grade. WARNING!!! This will only work once. It is expected that you will learn from this experience and read the directions/rubric more thoroughly the next time so the same thing doesn't happen again.

What if your school district doesn't have an online grade book? Teachers may provide progress reports or you may have to keep track on your own. Ask a teacher to help you or set up a table to record your own grades.

Keeping track of grades is great but remember the connection between effort and achievement? Don't believe that hard work pays off? You can use the following rubric to honestly rate your own effort on assignments or projects. Keep track of

Cracking the System: Study Skills for Teens
By Luann Swim

these scores in your planner and see how they correlate to the grades you earn on your work.

Effort Rubric for Students*
4: I worked on the task until it was completed. I pushed myself to continue working on the task even when difficulties arose or a solution was not immediately evident. I viewed difficulties that arose as opportunities to strengthen my understanding
3: I worked on the task until it was completed. I pushed myself to continue working on the task even though difficulties arose or a solution was not immediately evident.
2: I put some effort into the task, but I stopped working when difficulties arose.
1: I put very little effort into the task.

*CLASSROOM INSTRUCTION THAT WORKS : RESEARCH-BASED STRATEGIES FOR INCREASING STUDENT ACHIEVEMENT by Robert J. Marzano. Copyright 2001 by MID-CONTINENT RESEARCH FOR EDUCATION AND LEARNING. Reproduced with permission of MID-CONTINENT RESEARCH FOR EDUCATION AND LEARNING in the format Other book via Copyright Clearance Center.

Depending on the goal(s) you set for yourself, checking grades may not be enough. If your goal was to complete and turn in all of your homework, you may be able to track this online as well. Or, you can use a planner to record and check off homework as it is completed and turned in. (see the section on

Cracking the System: Study Skills for Teens
By Luann Swim

Homework Helps and using a planner for more information.) Some planners have specific spots for weekly or monthly goals; all planners can be used to track goals and their completion. How you use your planner is up to you. Along with writing down your homework, you can record your effort, and then your grade. You'll notice sections on using a planner in every chapter that follows; give some of the tips a try and see what works best for you!

CELEBRATE YOUR SUCCESS

Hooray! You reached your goal. Now what? Well, before you do anything else, think about how you feel about your accomplishment and yourself. Doesn't it feel great to have done something (mostly) on your own? Doesn't it give you a sense of satisfaction and pride? Don't you feel powerful-like you could do anything? These are the most important rewards you can give yourself. These are the feelings that will encourage and motivate you as a living, working adult. Feel great about yourself because of what you've done, on your own.

Cracking the System: Study Skills for Teens
By Luann Swim

Now that you feel great, come up with a tangible (something you can see, do, or touch) reward for yourself. Go to a movie or treat yourself to one of your favorites: food, video game, movie, etc. By giving **yourself** a reward, you are still accomplishing your goals for yourself. Don't get caught up in making grades for cash or for rewards from your parents. Take a step toward independence and do it because it's part of **your** plan for **your** future.

But what if you didn't reach your goal? Remember Michael Jordan's attitude toward failure and learn from this experience and try again. Maybe you need help from someone else. It takes courage to admit that you need help.

Remember, even presidents have a cabinet of advisors and superstars have agents. Find an adult you trust and ask them to help you reach your goals. There are lots of tips in the rest of this book that may help you. Read on...

Cracking the System: Study Skills for Teens
By Luann Swim

ORGANIZATION

BE PREPARED

What does the Boy Scout motto, "Be Prepared," have to do with study skills? You don't usually need to know how to make a campfire or do first aid to do well in school. But the founder of scouting, Robert Baden-Powell, had something much bigger in mind: be prepared for life, ready for any struggles or challenges it might throw at you. A wise young college student once told me that the most important thing she learned in middle school and early high school was how to take charge of her own learning-to be prepared.

Part of being organized is being prepared. You'll soon see that to *be prepared* looks different in different situations. But *be prepared* always has the ultimate goal of *be successful.* In this section of the book, *be prepare*d means to have all the supplies and materials you need to be successful. Schools publish supply lists in the summer and teachers include suggested materials and books on their

Cracking the System: Study Skills for Teens
By Luann Swim

course syllabi *(plural of syllabus, a course outline, which often includes materials, grading, and expectations).* Not only do you need the recommended supplies and materials at school, but it is very helpful to have a set at home as well. Some parents or students even buy their own copies of textbooks so they don't get left behind or to reduce the weight of backpacks. Let the supply list be your starting point and then consider some of the suggestions in the following sections to choose what will work for you.

USING A PLANNER

Learning to use a planner and then committing to use it is one of the most effective ways to start getting organized. Executive functions of the brain, like sense of time, organization, and working memory (keeping recently seen or heard information in memory) are essential in fulfilling responsibilities at home and school. Consistent use of a planner can help with all of these. Individuals with AD/HD may find particular benefit when using a planner

Cracking the System: Study Skills for Teens
By Luann Swim

effectively. Many adults, whether performers, athletes, or business professionals, use some type of planner to keep up with all of their responsibilities. Relying on a planner can really help make life easier and insure that you have time for everything in your busy life.

Many schools either supply or sell planners to their students. If your school offers a planner, learn to use it! These planners are often already organized by class subject and make homework/project tracking much easier. Teachers may refer to the planner and have tips on how to use it efficiently. If you need to find your own planner, make sure it has plenty of writing space for each day of the week and includes a smaller monthly calendar as well.

If you have tried using a planner and failed in the past, promise to give it one last serious try and consider finding a planner coach. This could be a teacher, counselor, or parent. Your coach should focus on your positive progress, give tips for

Cracking the System: Study Skills for Teens
By Luann Swim

improvement, and encourage you to reward yourself at the end of the week.

Here are some tips for using a planner:

1. Use your planner for everything! Start by recording sports practices, games, music lessons, rehearsals, etc.-anything that takes up part of your day.

2. Find a consistent place for your planner at school, in your backpack, and at home. At school, the corner of your desk, in a binder, or on top in your desk might be good locations. If your backpack has pockets, you might assign one to your planner only. At home, your planner should stay with your school materials, either in your backpack or in a binder. Wherever you decide to keep your planner, put it away in the same spot every day so you can always find it.

3. Refer to your planner regularly. Read it at home before you leave for school to make sure you have completed all assignments and

remember any appointments or special events. Write in it several times a day while at school, whenever you need to remember something. Check it before you leave school to make sure that you bring home any materials you need to complete your homework. And finally, refer to your planner when you do your homework.

4. Set up your planner for emergencies. Most planners have spaces for addresses and phone numbers. Record your parents' work or cell phone numbers, numbers for other trusted adults, your school number and/or attendance line. Think of your planner as your one-stop source of information!

5. Consider using your planner as your *Inspiration Station.* Ever have a great idea for a project, writing topic, song, etc. and then lose it later because you never wrote it down? Devote a *Notes* section of your planner to your great ideas.

Cracking the System: Study Skills for Teens
By Luann Swim

Thinking about using different pen/pencil colors for specific activities? Beware of turning your planner into another distraction or time waster. Use a special color for fun events, if you wish, but only those you record at home. Do, however, make your planner personal and an expression of your interests. Decorate the outside (at home of course!) with stickers, photos, etc. to make your planner truly yours. If you like your planner, you are more likely to use it and keep it handy at all times.

You'll notice that planners will show up in every section of this book; it's that important. You'll get specific tips on using your planner in class, for homework, and even for tests.

TOOLS OF THE TRADE

Each job has a required set of tools: guitar and microphone for a musician, football and helmet for an athlete, and script and props for an actor. Students require a set of tools as well. We've already discussed the importance of your planner in keeping organized. Your teacher or school most

Cracking the System: Study Skills for Teens
By Luann Swim

likely also gave you a list of required or recommended supplies. These are things you need to have at all times, both at school and at home. Even though your teacher made a good guess about how many pencils, erasers, pens, etc. you would need, it is **your** responsibility to keep track of your supplies and replenish them as needed. If you are running short of pencils or have lost your calculator, you need to replace them. (Use your planner to record what you need!)You can't do your job if you don't have the tools you need. If you don't have money for more school supplies, let your teacher or counselor know; they usually can find you the supplies you need.

You also need supplies to complete your homework. First, find a place in your home where you can keep your materials so they are easy to find but won't disappear. Try the desk in your room, a special spot on a bookcase, a drawer, even a box that slides under your bed. Set up a 3 ring *Homework Binder* with the following contents:

Cracking the System: Study Skills for Teens
By Luann Swim

- Zipper pouch with pencils, pens, sharpener, eraser, colored pencils, highlighter, calculator, protractor, scissors, sticky notes, and markers.
- All the types of paper you might need: notebook, graph, printer, or anything else specified by your teacher.
- A divider for each subject or class with a copy of the course syllabus, calendar, or other general information.
- Copies of instructions or rubrics for recurring assignments, like book reports, current events reports, essays, etc. filed in the appropriate section.
- Copies of instructions or rubrics for important projects that require significant work outside of school, filed in the appropriate section.
- Any other general "helps" like a list of commonly misspelled words, a conversion

chart for weights and measures, a general writing rubric, map of the world, etc.

- You might find that page protectors are helpful for keeping non-punched papers or important papers together.

This binder will give you just about all the materials you need to complete any routine homework assignment without spending valuable time hunting for a sharpened pencil. (If you don't like homework, the last thing you want to do is spend more time at it than needed!) Some other resources that could prove useful can either be in printed form or should be set up as favorites on your computer: dictionary, thesaurus and world atlas. If you don't have access to a computer all the time, try finding these resources at a used book store. You don't really need new copies and REUSE is a green concept.

Keep all your tools together and put them away when you're done. Replenish them as needed. The time you save will be worth it!

Cracking the System: Study Skills for Teens
By Luann Swim

TRANSPORT AND STORAGE:-

BACKPACKS AND LOCKERS

Backpacks seem more a fashion statement these days than a way to stay organized. However, the best backpack does both. You need to be willing to be seen with your backpack every day, so it's got to look good, but if your cool backpack doesn't fit your stuff, it's kind of useless. Although backpack needs will vary depending on your grade level, look for the following features in your backpack: back padding, padded straps, and belts at the waist to avoid back strain, a large compartment to fit folders, a standard size binder, and your lunch if you carry one, and enough other pockets or compartments to carry a pencil pouch, water bottle, cell phone, or other essential items. Look for durable fabric and zippers so the backpack makes it through the year.

Make sure the backpack gets completely emptied at least once a day, either at school or, preferably, at home. A backpack is transport, not a

Cracking the System: Study Skills for Teens
By Luann Swim

home away from home. If you empty it every day, there will be no collection of dirty gym clothes, moldy lunch, and crumpled papers at the bottom. Five minutes to empty your backpack every day is well worth it and just think of all the parent nagging you'll avoid. Hmmmm.... responsible for yourself. What a concept.

Lockers are the biggest source of anxiety for lots of middle school or junior high students. Will I remember my combination? What if I can't get it open? This anxiety fades quickly and the locker often becomes an extension of the student's room at home, tidy or messy. BEWARE the out of control locker, however. A locker that becomes a dumping ground can quickly consume homework, important information for parents, social announcements, and even whole books or textbooks.

Locker visits are usually brief and must be effective. Organize your materials by daily schedule, with all your books and materials for the morning together and those for the afternoon in another spot.

Cracking the System: Study Skills for Teens
By Luann Swim

If you need to better organize the space, try out a locker shelf or divider. Or consider putting all the textbooks in one location and binders, folders, and notebooks in another. Color-code your materials so they are easy to find. A well-organized locker can help you avoid "tardies."

DEVELOPING A SYSTEM

We are all unique individuals, with different strengths and weaknesses, different interests and abilities. So it should come as no surprise that there is no one-size-fits-all organization system. Taking personal responsibility and then being deliberate and consistent in becoming organized is an important first step. For years I was plagued by lost keys: I was ready to leave the house and couldn't find my keys, often reverting to the set of "extras" in the drawer. My husband, probably driven crazy by this repeated performance, suggested I hang them on a hook on the refrigerator every time I came home. That was a great suggestion, but until I acknowledged that I needed to change and deliberately and consistently tried out this system, it was only someone else's idea. I added my own second part to this system and found a special pocket in my purse for my keys when I was away from home. Now this is **my** system for managing my keys. Even after years of practice, I still need to make the effort and be consistent in applying this system for it to work.

The same may be true for you. Organization may not come naturally for you. It may take a few trials before you find systems that work for you. The following sections will help you to organize and make the most of your classroom, homework, and tests.

CLASSROOM STRATEGIES

BE PREPARED

Time to think like a Boy Scout again. What does it mean to be prepared in class? You could probably get an answer to this from a younger elementary student. "It means I have my materials on my desk and I am quiet and ready to learn." Not too much changes as you get older. This is still the

Cracking the System: Study Skills for Teens
By Luann Swim

essence of being prepared in the classroom with just a few additions.

Here's a big one that teens really don't like to hear: get more sleep! Even 30-60 minutes of lost sleep can influence brain function, causing a two year decline in academic performance. Teen brains are still developing and lack of sleep may cause permanent changes in brain structure. Studies connect longer sleep times to higher academic performance. Your brain processes the previous day's learning and information while you sleep. In addition, tired brains do not process information as well and memory suffers. Want to do your best in school? Give yourself a fighting chance and get eight hours of sleep.

The human brain accounts for about 2% of total body weight yet uses 20-30% of the total energy used by the body. There's a long time between dinner and breakfast and even longer till lunchtime.

Cracking the System: Study Skills for Teens
By Luann Swim

Do your brain a favor and eat a good breakfast, with some protein, carbs, and fat, before heading off to school.

Now that you're all fueled up with sleep and food, its time to go back to being prepared like a second grader. Before you get to class make sure you have all the materials you need: notebook, paper, pencils, etc. By this stage in your school career you can figure out what you need most of the time. If you need something special you can count on your teacher to let you know. The last thing you need is your planner at the ready.

Even though this is the last thing discussed, it is the most important thing to get ready. Check your attitude. If you expect to learn, you will. If you enter with the attitude that you either know it all, school is pointless, or this is social hour, that is what you will get from your time in class. Your attitude is everything and is completely under your control. Choose well.

Cracking the System: Study Skills for Teens
By Luann Swim

ACTIVE LISTENING

When you checked your attitude, you began the first step of active listening: be focused. At best, we may only remember 25-50% of what we hear so it's really important to pay attention! Listen for reminders about homework or upcoming projects or tests and then for an introduction to the subject you will be learning. Access your background knowledge on this subject, either from a previous class or your own personal information. You will remember more if your brain can make connections between what you already know and new information. Help your brain out by consciously making these connections.

You are actively listening when your eyes are focused on the speaker. Avoid possible distractions like looking out the window, talkative classmates, or "stuff" on your desk. You should still be able to keep eye contact most of the time, even while taking notes, the subject of our next section.

The last step in active listening requires clarifying, making clear, what you've heard. You can do this by asking questions or restating what you heard in your own words. For example, if the teacher says, "Kangaroos are marsupials, like koalas and wombats that carry their babies in a pouch," you could clarify by stating or asking, "So, marsupials are animals that carry their young in a pouch?"

Try to make some connections here too. You could ask, "Are there any other marsupials that I might know?" or "Is carrying babies in a pouch a little like hatching an egg?"

Good listening is an important skill to practice while you are in school. Listening skills are in great demand in the business world. Businesses and professionals spend lots of money trying to teach themselves the art of active listening. Get a head start!

NOTE-TAKING STRATEGIES

Middle school and high school signal the beginning of serious note taking in school. Teacher lectures and individual text reading nearly demand notes, unless one has a photographic memory. In addition, research has identified note taking, when combined with summarizing, as a highly effective instructional strategy, one that can boost student achievement in all grade levels, on average, as much as 34%. While not every student or every note taking experience is guaranteed to get these results, effective note taking and summarizing are certainly worth exploring as viable study skills. As with organization, however, note taking styles vary and may need to be changed to suit a particular subject or student.

When should you take notes? If you've been assigned a book report, you should take notes that will support the report while reading your book. A handy way to record information is on a modified bookmark. Use a folded piece of notebook paper, which gives you four separate columns to record information. For example, if you are analyzing a character in the book, you can record the character's words or actions, including the page number, and a word or words that describe the character (character

Cracking the System: Study Skills for Teens
By Luann Swim

trait). This bookmark format can be used for any type of book report from fiction to non-fiction. In order to use this, however, you must first decide a purpose for your reading, an essential strategy for any reading assignment.

If you are assigned reading in a textbook or informational article, you should be looking for the main ideas in the text and recording them in your notes. When your teacher is lecturing and giving important information about a topic or subject and writing points on the board, you should be taking your own notes. One useful format for both class/lecture notes and text reading is the Cornell Notes style, developed by Walter Pauk, an education professor at Cornell University. This note taking format is useful because it uses regular notebook paper and offers space for recording information while reading or listening and then is organized to encourage reflection and review of the material. The bottom of the page, five to six lines, is reserved for a summary, to be completed after your reading or

Cracking the System: Study Skills for Teens
By Luann Swim

class. The rest of the page is divided into two sections. The left-hand column should be about 2 ½ inches wide and the right section of the paper is used to take notes. You may want to prepare several pages ahead of time and have them ready in your binder. After a while, you will be able to organize your page without preparing pages ahead of time.

If you are reading a textbook or informational article, use the left column to turn the titles, subheadings, and/or topic sentences into questions and to record **bold** or *italicized* vocabulary words or concepts. Use the right column to write answers to the questions or definitions of the words. Use phrases, not complete sentences, to answer the questions. Use bullets to help organize your ideas. Use abbreviations or symbols to record information more efficiently. When you complete your reading, stop and reflect on what you've read. Using the bottom of the paper, write a brief summary of what you read, including the important main ideas. (Figure 1 shows a page of notes from a chemistry textbook)

Cracking the System: Study Skills for Teens
By Luann Swim

When you review these notes or are studying for a quiz, cover or fold the right side of the paper and aloud, to yourself, answer the questions or define the words in the left column. Check your answers using the notes in the right column. Reread the summary and make connections to the details you recorded in your notes. Speaking to yourself while studying allows your brain another way to capture the information and forge connections to other data, important to long-term storage and retrieval.

When taking notes in class, the format is the same, but the procedure is a little different. While in class, take notes in the right column only. Be sure to write anything that is on the board or that your teacher says is important or will be on the test. Use phrases and abbreviations, capturing main ideas instead of examples. As soon as possible after class, use the left column to generate questions based on the notes in the right-hand column. These will be a great help in preparing for quizzes or exams! Finally, use the bottom of the page to summarize the notes and record any questions to need to ask the next day in class.

While the Cornell Notes system works great for many, if you try it and it does not suit you, don't give up on note-taking. There are many other possible formats you can use. Talk to your teachers, counselor, or search online for note-taking strategies. Keep trying until you find one that works for you!

Both reading notes and class notes should be reviewed every week using the procedure described above. If you spend at least 15 minutes every week reviewing all your previous notes, you will remember more for class use and will be better prepared for quizzes and tests.

USING A PLANNER

While you are in class, your planner should be readily accessible, either on your desk or immediately at hand. At the bare minimum, use it to

Cracking the System: Study Skills for Teens
By Luann Swim

record any assignments or homework on their due dates. Even if you complete the work in class, record it anyway. If your planner has enough room, you could also record any reading you did in class, lab experiments, or the lesson topic. By using your planner in this way, you will have a complete record of all the learning activities that relate to the unit you are covering. When you get ready to study, you can locate all of these papers and review them prior to the quiz or test. Most teachers, contrary to popular student belief, plan class activities to support learning. By reviewing all of these activities you will have a complete overview of the information that is important to remember or understand.

HOMEWORK HELPS

BE PREPARED AND USE YOUR PLANNER

Homework is meant to be practice of concepts already learned at school. So the first way to be prepared to do your homework is to pay attention and try your best in the classroom. Ask questions if

Cracking the System: Study Skills for Teens
By Luann Swim

you don't understand while you are in class; this will make completing your homework much easier.

Record all homework and projects in your planner on the day they are due. Many teachers post homework somewhere in their classrooms or on a web page. Get in the habit of checking that location every day. Even if you complete your homework in class, still record it in your planner. Use a check (☑) to indicate you already finished this assignment. By recording all homework in your planner, you will have a complete record of the work you've done for any study unit. When it is time to prepare for a test, you will know what to review.

For long term projects or assignments, record on the due date but be aware that you may need additional planner reminders along the way to complete the assignment. In the section "Turning It In" we'll talk about how to break a big assignment into smaller pieces so you aren't overwhelmed at the last minute.

Cracking the System: Study Skills for Teens
By Luann Swim

The next challenge is getting your homework home. There are several options here. The simplest is a trick you should have learned in elementary school: use a homework folder. This can be a pocket folder that travels with you all day long, maybe inside or along with your planner. Put any assignments, instructions, or resources into this folder as soon as homework is assigned. At the end of the day, you can look through this folder and decide which textbooks or other materials you might need to bring home to help with your homework. One folder to take homework home and one folder to bring it back-simple. Another possibility is to use pocket dividers for your 3-ring binder. You can use one side of the pocket to take homework home and the other pocket to return it to school. This option might be good if you tend to forget to bring information home that lives in your binder, but it does add considerable weight to your backpack.

Being prepared at home means you have everything you need to complete an assignment.

Cracking the System: Study Skills for Teens
By Luann Swim

Refer back to the Organization chapter to make sure you have all the tools and papers you need to complete your homework. Keeping everything in one place means you don't waste time looking for your materials. Don't make doing homework take longer than it should!

TIME AND PLACE

Getting your homework done efficiently and accurately requires concentration. Many teens insist that they can do homework while watching TV or texting or monitoring their social networking page. If you want your homework to take all night and then get a poor grade, continue this practice. Just as states are considering banning texting while driving, ban it and other distractions during your homework time.

You will need to look at your own schedule and decide on the best time for **you** to do your homework. If you need a break after school, take it and begin your homework later. Don't want to miss favorite TV shows in the evening? Finish your

Cracking the System: Study Skills for Teens
By Luann Swim

homework as soon as you get home. Find the time best for you and then stick to it. Start by working for 30 minutes, without distractions, and then take a break for 5-10 minutes. A good break might mean a snack or some physical activity to get your blood flowing to your body and brain. Increase your work time up to an hour if that works for you. But if you are facing hours of homework, don't eliminate breaks. They will keep you alert and efficient. Even if you have no written homework, use your homework time daily to review notes, assignments, class work, and reading to insure that this new information is being stored in your long-term memory. This daily review will pay off when it comes time to prepare for quizzes and tests!

Finding a place to do homework is a lot like finding a time-it must suit **you.** Some people work best at a desk or table or at the library. Others can lounge on the floor or a bed. Be honest with yourself and find a place where you can eliminate distractions and really concentrate. After all, you are not doing

Cracking the System: Study Skills for Teens
By Luann Swim

this for your parents. You are doing this for you. If you choose the wrong time or place you are only hurting yourself. Your homework will take longer and your grades will be lower. Isn't it worth it to turn your phone off for 30 minutes if you can get your homework done more quickly (and accurately)?

CSIQ

C omplete

S entence

I ncluding the

Q uestion

> Why did the author choose to write in this style?
>
> The author chose this writing style because ...

If you have never learned this acronym, now is the time. It is a good one to use when completing your homework or taking a test. When you are asked to write answers to questions, get in the habit of writing in complete sentences (which state a complete thought with a subject/noun/ and what that subject is doing/verb). Your sentence should use part of the question in the answer so that anyone reading your answer actually knows the question without reading it. When you spend time doing homework, it pays to do it thoroughly.

HELP! I DON'T GET IT!

You need to be prepared for the time when you are stuck and need help with your homework. Just about everybody faces this problem sooner or later. First, make sure you have the phone number of at least one responsible person in your class. Ask them specifically if it would be OK if you called with questions from class. (This is also a nice way to meet new people!) Use this person to check due dates, details on assignments, or even to provide a copy of worksheets. (Think scan and email for the easiest solution!) Be careful, however, about getting help with content unless you are certain that this person knows what they are doing.

It would be great if you had reviewed the homework assignment before leaving school and asked all your questions of your teacher, but this doesn't always happen. You can try getting help from your parents but remember that it is a long time

Cracking the System: Study Skills for Teens
By Luann Swim

since they were in your grade and expectations and methods sometimes change. If you are unable to get help from a friend or parent, check out other resources. Libraries sometimes offer homework assistance, by partnering with high school honor students or a local college. Online resources might be another place to look. A good place to start is your school or teacher's website or page. Next, try your local library webpage. Be careful if you are using a search engine to find help; just because someone has a webpage doesn't mean they are qualified to help you. Once you find a good resource, put it in your favorites so you can easily find it again.

If you consistently have questions about homework in a particular subject, seek out your teacher's "tutor time" or office hours. Perhaps some one-on-one help will give you the jump-start you need to become more independent. Or, think about finding a small group of friends for a homework group. Many times, even kids who are struggling a bit can help each other in different ways. For example, maybe all the group members find writing to be challenging overall but one is a great speller, one really understands grammar and organization, and another has a creative vocabulary. By combining these strengths, some really awesome writing can happen. Keep in mind that you are working together to help yourself learn, not just to get an assignment done. Copying homework is a temporary solution that only creates more problems.

TURNING IT IN

Too many kids spend all kinds of time completing their homework and then earn incompletes because they forget or neglect to turn it in! If turning your homework in is a particular problem for you, you may want to use a double check system in your planner: one check indicates completed homework, the second check means it was turned in. Even if you are uncertain about the quality or did not have time to finish, turn your work

Cracking the System: Study Skills for Teens
By Luann Swim

in on time. You can always add a note that you were unclear about the assignment, ran out of time, etc. At least your teacher knows that you tried and may give you additional time or help to finish the work. Just like with redoing assignments to improve your grade, however, don't try this more than once or your teacher will quickly discover that you are just making up excuses. Use the homework folder to take your completed assignments back to school or place your completed work in a pocket of your divider. Teachers are not very impressed by rumpled papers from the bottom of your backpack. If you are taking the time to do your homework, take pride in how it looks as well.

Now, what about long-term projects that seem to suddenly be due tomorrow? If your teacher has not broken down the project for you, set some short-term goals for yourself and, if needed, ask your teacher to spot check your progress as you go along. Do you need to create a journal of the Lewis and Clark expedition with maps, journal entries, notes, and a works cited page, all due in 3 weeks? Do your research the first week, taking Cornell notes, and create your maps or a special journal entry. Focus on getting the bulk of the journal entries done the second week. In the final week, prepare your works cited page and review and complete the rest of the assignment. Along the way, you can be checking with your teacher, sharing your progress and making sure you are on the right track. Record each step in your planner with your **own** due date, to make sure you are making progress. Only you know the details of your personal schedule so you may need to work ahead to fit in that soccer championship that comes up right before your project is due. That's another good reason for using your planner for everything that's going on in your life.

Finally, even if you miss the due date on an assignment and your grade will suffer, complete the work and turn it in as soon as possible. Homework is meant to support your learning and if you simply skip part of the work, your understanding of the subject will suffer and know that it **will** show up on a quiz or test.

TESTS-STUDY AND STRATEGIES

As with completing homework, you will be prepared to take tests when you have done your best to pay attention in class and complete your in-class and homework assignments. Taking notes during class and when you read articles or textbooks can also be a big help. The last important piece is the daily review of concepts learned; this sets things up in your memory for later recall. Most of your preparation for a test should take place every day as you learn, practice, and review material. This strong daily effort means you don't need to "cram" or "pull an all nighter" to get ready for a test.

USING A PLANNER

Record dates of quizzes and tests in your planner as soon as they are announced. Three to five days before the quiz or test, schedule a study session by writing it in your planner. Make an appointment with yourself to study so you don't forget. Depending on how your first study session goes, plan additional sessions up until the quiz or test to help memorize or review material.

STUDY TIPS

Studying for an end of unit quiz is a lot different from studying for a final exam. But some general study tips will apply in all situations. First, make sure to study when you are "fresh." Be wide awake and free of distractions. Several short study sessions when you are really focused are better than one big marathon. Vary the style of your study to engage all your learning styles: read text or notes (visual), repeat or sing information to yourself (oral), use your body to tap, dance, or catch while reviewing (kinesthetic), or reorganize information by creating a model, chart, or picture (visual/spatial).

When reviewing reading, it is more efficient to study notes than to reread whole chapters. Didn't take notes? In a textbook, look for a chapter review and quiz yourself and/or find answers in the text. No

Cracking the System: Study Skills for Teens
By Luann Swim

chapter review? Use the headings and topic sentences as hints to summarize the text. List words in bold and quiz yourself about their meanings and check your answers in the glossary.

MEMORY TIPS

Memorizing things like terms, elements, math facts, vocabulary, etc. requires different techniques. Try fitting information into a song or rhythm to help you remember, like the A-B-C song. Make memory cards and post them in places you visit often (like the mirror, bathroom, or refrigerator), reading them each time you visit. Use drive time as review time: ask your driver/parent to quiz you. Practice your sport and memorize at the same time: kick soccer goals while repeating math facts, spell words while playing catch, or review vocabulary while passing a football. Develop an acronym or acrostic to help remember items in a series like **P**LEASE **E**XCUSE **M**Y **D**EAR **A**UNT **S**ALLY for the order of operations (parentheses, exponents, multiplication, division, addition, subtraction) in math. The more ways you experience something, the better chance it has of being put into your long-term memory. These memorization techniques can provide "hooks" for retrieving those memories.

Consider getting together with other students to study for important exams or tests. Make sure before you begin, however, that everyone in your group is serious about studying! You can use this opportunity to quiz each other and to explain what you know to someone else. "Teaching" someone else requires a full understanding and is great preparation for a test.

TEST TAKING TIPS

One of the best ways to get ready for a test is to have your mind and body in top shape. Make sure you have plenty of sleep, eight hours are best, and be sure to eat a balanced meal as suggested in the Be Prepared section of Classroom Strategies. Engaging in some physical activity that gets your heart pumping will help insure a good blood supply to your most important test taking organ, your brain.

Cracking the System: Study Skills for Teens
By Luann Swim

If you have ever suffered from test anxiety, you know that feeling anxious or nervous interferes with doing your best. If you have followed all or some of the note-taking or study suggestions in this book, know that you are well prepared and use this to help yourself relax. Try slow, deep, rhythmic breathing while telling yourself that you are equipped to handle the test. While others crammed last minute for college finals, I used to take a bubble bath to relax! Feeling relaxed and confident can make a big difference.

When you begin a test, make sure you read the directions carefully. Look over the whole test quickly to get an idea of what you will need to complete. If the test is very long and you anticipate you will not finish, either find the part of the test with the most points and work on that first or find a section that will be easy for you and complete that. It is generally best to answer the questions you know first. Skip those you aren't sure about and come back to them. Sometimes working out answers to other questions can help. You may also find hints within the test itself.

Be sure to read questions carefully. Make sure you know what the question is asking before you answer. You may even want to underline part of the question to focus your answer. If the question asks what **percent** of the class of 32 students and you answer "4 students," your response clearly does not answer the question.

Some tips for specific types of questions: Put fill-in-the-blank answers into the statement and read to yourself silently. Does it make sense or sound right? Even if you don't **know** the answer, increase your chance of success by eliminating multiple choice responses you know are wrong. Use the CSIQ format to provide short answers.

When you finish your test, take time to review your answers. Reread questions to make sure you have answered the question asked. Proofread written responses to ensure your answer makes sense as written; check for spelling or grammatical errors. Don't second guess all of your answers, however, because often your first, gut response is correct.

What if you run out of time? Many teachers will offer extended time if you ask. Just make sure that you are asking for time to finish, not time to ask others for answers. Cheating is a lousy way to pass a test or class. There is no sense of accomplishment, very little has been learned that will help in future classes or life, and it's unfair to everyone else.

CONCLUSION

By now I'm sure you realize that there are no shortcuts to success in school. It takes hard work and effort. So, after reading this book I hope you are ready to try some new things to help you succeed. You are unique in your strengths and weaknesses and will need to determine your best starting point. If organization is a problem for you, start there, it is really the foundation of all the rest. Commit yourself to consistent daily effort in paying attention in class,

Cracking the System: Study Skills for Teens
By Luann Swim

completing homework, and review of material.

Remember, you are in charge and can make a

difference in your success at school.

References

Bronson, Po. "Snooze or Lose." *New York* 08 Oct 2007: n. pag. Web. 09 Sept 2009. <http://nymag.com/news/features/38951/index4.html>.

Marzano, Robert, Debra Pickering, and Jane Pollock. *Classroom Instruction that Works*. Alexandria, VA: ASCD, 2001. Print.

Pauk, Walter. "The Cornell Note-Taking System." *Cornell University Learning Strategies Center*. Cornell University, Web. 22 Sept 2009. <http://lsc.sas.cornell.edu/Sidebars/Study_Skills_Resources/cornellsystem.pdf

"Time Management: Learning to Use a Day Planner." *National Resource Center on AD/HD:*. May 2003. National Resource Center on AD/HD:, Web. 21 Sept 2009. <http://www.help4adhd.org/en/living/organdtime/WWK11>.

Cracking the System: Study Skills for Teens
By Luann Swim

ORDER FORM
Name_____Address_____
                                                                  Street Number and Name

City:_____State:_____Zip Code:_____

Email Address:_____
I would like to order _____copies of *Cracking The System*, by Luann Swim.
You may charge my credit card for $19.95 for each book, plus $4.50 shipping.
My credit card number is_____
Exp. Date:_____Sec. Code:_____
$19.95 for _____   *Books* = $_____
       Number   *Shipping* + $4.50._____

Total Amount to be charged: $_____
I authorize the total amount, above, to be charged to the above credit card.

_____Date_____
Signature
Please mail the above order form to:
B& B Educational Advancement & Publications, Inc.
1407 Ford Street, Golden, Colorado 80401
Or you may order your book on the website at
      www.bbeapublications .com

www.ingramcontent.com/pod-product-compliance
Lightning Source LLC
Chambersburg PA
CBHW080744250426
43671CB00038B/2861